Reduce, Reuse, and Recycle

by Margie Burton, Cathy French, and Tammy Jones

Table of Contents

Where Does All of Our Garbage Go?

We all make garbage. Where does all of our garbage go? Some things are put into trash bins to be thrown away into a big landfill of garbage.

The landfills are getting full because the garbage just stays there. Some landfills are so big that they look like mountains.

The garbage goes into landfills.

What Kind of Garbage Can Make the Soil Better?

Does all of the garbage that you make have to go to a landfill? No! You can use some of the garbage again to make the soil better. You can make compost from grass clippings and other dead plants.

She is putting grass clippings into a compost pile.

You can use some other garbage from the house in the compost bin. Some egg shells and peelings from fruit can be put into the compost bin.

You can put some worms into the compost bin to help make soil. The worms eat old leaves and other plants and leave behind soil in which new plants can grow.

How Can You Use Garbage Again and Again?

Do you have some old newspapers, soda cans,
or plastic bottles and bags? They
can be put into bins to be used
again and again.

You recycle when you use something again.
These children are taking the cans to
the recycling center so that they can be used again.

You can get soda cans, foil, and tin pie plates and take them to be used again. You will get some money if you do!

1. Wash the can.

2. Smash the can.

3. Place the can in a bag.

4. Take the bag to the recycling place.

5. Get some money for the cans.

Can you use old newspapers again and again? Yes! You can use them to make some new paper.

1. Tear the paper into little bits.

4. Add 2 tablespoons of corn starch.

7. Place it between some newspapers.

2. Put some water
   on the paper.

3. Beat it with
   an eggbeater.

5. Pour the mix into
   a flat pan.

6. Use a screen
   to lift it.

8. Roll it with a jar to
   get the water out.

9. Peel it off when
   it is dry.

How Can You Keep Garbage Out of Landfills?

You can help keep garbage out of landfills by using things again and again. Things that can be used again and again have this sign.

You keep garbage out of landfills when you recycle.